Secular H^{What *Is*}umanism?

Secular HWhat *Is* Humanism?

by Paul Kurtz

Published for

CENTER
FOR
INQUIRY
Transnational

Amherst, New York 14226

Prometheus Books
59 John Glenn Drive
Amherst, New York 14228-2197
www.prometheusbooks.com

Published 2007 by Prometheus Books

Inquiries should be addressed to
Prometheus Books
59 John Glenn Drive
Amherst, New York 14228-2197
VOICE: 716-691-0133, ext. 207 • FAX: 716-564-2711
www.prometheusbooks.com

15 14 13 12 11   5 4 3 2

Library of Congress-in-Publication Data

Kurtz, Paul, 1925–
    What is secular humanism? / by Paul Kurtz.
        p. cm.
    Includes bibliographical references and index.
    ISBN: 978–1–59102–499–6
    1. Secularism. 2. Humanism. I. Title.

BL2747.8.K87 2007
211'.6—dc22
                                                    2006052885

TABLE OF CONTENTS

PREFACE

Are there any ethical values and principles that nonreligious individuals can live by? In a time when many have forsaken other-worldly religions, what does human life

mean? What is its significance? Secular humanism attempts to answer these questions in a way that resonates with human aspirations and the findings of science. It provides a scientific, philosophical, and ethical outlook that exerts a profound influence on civilization and that may be traced back to the ancient world, through the modern world, down to the present. Today many schools of thought broadly identify with humanist ideas and values. By conjoining the term *secular* with *humanism,* we may narrow its focus and meaning, enabling us to distinguish secular humanism from other forms of humanism, particularly religious humanism.

Succinctly, secular humanism rejects supernatural accounts of reality; but it seeks to optimize the fullness of human life in a naturalistic universe. Secular humanism and modernism have often been considered as synonymous, for secular humanism finds meaning in this life here and now and expresses confidence in the power of human beings to solve their problems and conquer uncharted frontiers, the theme of the modern world of exploration and discovery. In the contemporary world, however, secular humanism affirms a bold *new paradigm* that weaves together many historical threads, but adds much more that is relevant to the rapidly emerging planetary civilization.

HISTORY

Classical Roots

Secular humanism traces its heritage back to Confucian China, to the Carvaka materialist movement in ancient India, and to the writers, artists, and poets of ancient Greece and Rome. Its origins can be glimpsed in early Greek philosophy, especially in its efforts to develop a theoretical philosophical and scientific outlook on nature, in its emphasis on rationality, and in its conviction that the good life can be achieved through the exercise of human powers and the fulfillment of human nature. Protagoras stands out as a humanist, in view of his statement that "man is the measure of all things." However, humanistic strains can be seen in other Greek philosophers: the Sophists, who attacked conventional morality and sought

Socrates

Aristotle

new ethical standards, as well as Socrates and Plato, who rejected the Homeric myths and sought to base ethics on rational inquiry.

Aristotle's *Nicomachean Ethics* has been taken as a model of humanistic ethics, as it champions the life of practical wisdom, the fulfillment of virtue and excellence, and the achievement of well-being. Roman philosophy also expressed humanistic values: this was especially true of epicureanism (Epicurus and Lucretius), stoicism (Epictetus and Marcus Aurelius), and skepticism (Carneades, Pyrrho, and Sextus Empiricus).

Humanism was eclipsed during the Dark Ages, during which faith dominated Western culture and humans looked vainly outside of themselves to a deity for salvation. Humanism began to reappear with the re-discovery and translation by the Islamic philosopher Averröes of the works of Aristotle in the twelfth century, and their transmission to Europe during the Middle Ages.

Galileo

MODERN SECULAR HUMANISM

It was during the Renaissance, beginning in the fourteenth century—when there was a turning away from the Bible back to classical pagan virtues, and an effort to secularize morality—that humanism began to flourish again as a literary and philosophical movement. Writers emphasized that the good life and happiness were possible and that earthly pleasures were to be cultivated, not con-

Giordano Bruno

David Hume

Voltaire

demned. Gianozzo Manetti, Marsilio Ficino, and Giovanni Pico della Mirandola were philosophical humanists. They highlighted the dignity of human beings, their capacity for freedom, and the need for tolerance. Desiderius Erasmus of Holland was especially noted as a humanist because of his defense of religious tolerance.

The emergence of modern science in the sixteenth and seventeenth centuries enabled secular humanism to assume a recognizable form. Many thinkers helped to bring this outlook into being. For example, Michel de Montaigne expressed both skeptical and humanistic values. Benedict Spinoza, a bridge between the medieval and modern outlook, defended freethought, rejected biblical revelation as a source of ethics, paved the way for a new science of nature, and attempted to naturalize religion by identifying God with nature.

The first major protest by what we may recognize as modern secular humanism was the defense of freedom of inquiry against ecclesiastical and political censorship. In part because of this, secular humanism and freethought are closely identified in the modern world. The fates of Giordano Bruno, burned at the stake, and Galileo Galilei, shamed and sentenced to house arrest, for challenging traditional views of the cosmos are central to the humanist call for freedom.

It was the development of the scientific method and its applica-

Thomas Paine

Thomas Jefferson

tion to nature that brought a decisive intellectual influence to bear on humanist thought. Humanists wished to use reason (as with René Descartes) or experience (as with Sir Francis Bacon, John Locke, and David Hume) to account for natural processes and discover causal laws. This meant that appeals to the authority of religious revelation and tradition were held illegitimate as a source of knowledge.

The scientific revolution began with the impressive development of physics, astronomy, and natural philosophy. The Enlightenment, or Age of Reason, is testimony to humanist efforts to extend the methods of reason and science to the study of society and the human being. In the eighteenth and nineteenth centuries there was widespread confidence that with the spread of reason, science, and education, human beings could be liberated from superstition and build a better world. Thinkers like Condorcet set forth a progressive prospectus for humanity. Deists were critical of clericalism, rejected appeals to biblical revelation, and sought to develop a religion of nature and reason. Significant figures include Voltaire, Denis Diderot, and the Baron D'Holbach. Also in the modern period, democratic revolutions proclaimed "liberty," "equality," and "fraternity," and heralded "life, liberty, and the pursuit of happiness." Humanists defended the ideals of freedom against a repressive government or church, insisted on tolerance for opposing viewpoints, and championed a belief in the right of free conscience and dissent. Utilitarians including Jeremy Bentham, James Mill, and John Stuart Mill continued these trends in the nineteenth century, judging legislation by its effect on the common good.

SECULARISM

Along with the growth of humanism has come the growth of secularist ideals. The modern world has witnessed the widespread secularization of life. This means first that morality could be freed from religious authorities. The values and ideals of reason, freedom, happiness, and social justice would be substituted for the virtues of faith, hope, and charity—and for an exaggerated sense of sin. Second, secularization involved an effort to limit ecclesiastical control over the various institutions of society, especially the state, the schools, and the economy. Fear of an established church led to the principle of the separation of church and state, embodied in the First Amendment to the U. S. Constitution. It derives its authority from "We the People," not God. Thomas Jefferson, Thomas Paine, Benjamin Franklin, James Madison, and other leaders of the American Revolution were deeply influenced by secular and humanist ideals.

CONTEMPORARY SECULAR HUMANISM

In the nineteenth and twentieth centuries a growing number of thinkers (Karl Marx,

> **"Secular humanism is avowedly non-religious. It is a eupraxsophy (good practical wisdom), which draws its basic principles and ethical values from science, ethics, and philosophy"**

Sigmund Freud, Albert Camus, Bertrand Russell, John Dewey, George Santayana,

Alfred J. Ayer, and Sidney Hook) and movements (Marxism, existentialism, pragmatism, naturalism, positivism, behaviorism, libertarianism, and others) have claimed humanist credentials. Forms of humanism that claim to be religious also proliferated, especially in the twentieth century. The term *humanism* is considered so ennobling that few thinkers are willing to reject it outright. Thus, the Roman Catholic philosopher Jacques Maritain referred to "Christian humanism" as a concern for ameliorating the human condition on earth, and maintained that Christian humanism is the most authentic form of humanism. Liberal

Bertrand Russell

John Dewey

Simone de Beauvoir

Jean-Paul Sartre

unitarian-universalism also fits under this rubric. Religious humanists introduced a distinction between a "religion" and the supposed "religious" qualities of experience, and choose to emphasize the latter. They considered "God" not as an independently existing entity but as a human expression of the highest ideals (Dewey) or of our "ultimate concern" (Paul Tillich). Such attempts at redefinition are generally nontheistic.

In contemporary society secular humanism has been singled out by critics and proponents alike as a position sharply distinguishable from any religious formulation. Religious fundamentalists in the United States have waged a campaign against secular humanism, claiming that it is a rival "religion" and seeking to root it out from American public life. Secular humanism is avowedly *non*-religious. It is a *eupraxsophy* (good practical wisdom), which draws its basic principles and ethical values from science, ethics, and philosophy.

In the late twentieth century the papacy of John Paul II had abandoned the reformist agenda of the Second Vatican Council (Vatican II, 1962-65), which had expressed many humanist values. In the early twenty-first century, Pope Benedict XVI rejected "secularism" and "relativism," which he considered to be purely subjective. Islam has likewise vigorously opposed secularism, many adherents insisting that Muslim law (*Sharia*) is rooted in the Qur'an. Muslim extremists have defended theocracy rather than democracy, and they have even threatened *jihad* against those who espouse the secular outlook and champion freedom of conscience. Following Heidegger, many French postmodernist philosophers have likewise rejected humanism, along with any notion that science can be objective or that science and technology can provide the basis for a philosophy or ideology of emancipation. It should be noted, however, that other French thinkers held dissenting positions. Jean-Paul Sartre argued that existentialism *was* a humanism; Simone de Beauvoir constructed an emancipatory defense of the rights of women rooted firmly in humanist principles. Contemporary secular humanists have been highly critical of postmodernism for its rejection of modernism, its pessimism, and its Nihilism about the human prospect.

A NEW PARADIGM

Secular humanism provides a comprehensive synthesis of several key intellectual and ethical trends in world civilization. This new paradigm draws from freethought and rationalism, atheism and agnosticism, skepticism and unbelief. Yet it goes beyond these historic movements by crafting a new outlook relevant to contemporary times. It has sometimes been taken as negative because it criticizes the sacred cows of society; but it actually delivers a positive ethical message that has significant pragmatic consequences for human culture. It presents affirmative alternatives to the reigning orthodoxies.

The secular humanist paradigm has six main characteristics: (1) it is a method of inquiry, (2) it provides a naturalistic cosmic outlook, (3) it is nontheistic, (4) it is committed to humanistic ethics, (5) it offers a perspective that is democratic, and (6) it is planetary in scope. I should point out that many allies within the freethought or rationalist movement may accept one or more of these characteristics without accepting them all. Some mistakenly consider secular humanism to be equivalent with atheism, others with methodological naturalism, and still others with humanistic ethics. Secular humanism, however, is broader than any of these views; for it provides an integrated scientific-philosophical synthesis that encom-

"Secular humanism proposes the complete implementation of the agenda of modernism... what is necessary for it to occur is a New Enlightenment."

passes all of these and more. This is sometimes called "naturalistic humanism." Ultimately, secular humanism proposes nothing less than the complete implementation of the agenda of modernism. This agenda in fact has yet to be fully implemented; what is necessary for it to occur is a *post-postmodernist* New Enlightenment.

METHOD OF INQUIRY

Secular humanism relies on the methods of science to test claims to truth. This is known as *methodological naturalism,* the cornerstone of modern science. Broadly conceived, it is the hypothetical-deductive method, in which hypotheses are tested by their experimental effects and predictive power, integrated into theories, and validated by their comprehensive character and mathematical elegance. The grounds of a hypothesis are open to anyone who can examine the evidence and the reasons for its support. These can be objectively corroborated by independent inquirers. On this interpretation, the scientific method is no esoteric arcane art available only to a narrow coterie of disciples; nor does it lay down fixed rules of investigation. Rather, it is continuous with ordinary common sense or critical intelligence, and it involves the controlled use of the methods of inquiry that are successful in other areas of life as well.

All human knowledge is fallible, all claims to ultimate or absolute truth questionable. Hypotheses should be taken as tentative, for even well-established principles may later be modified in the light of new evidence or more comprehensive explanations. Thus the scientific method entails some degree of skepticism, but this is not of a negative character, denying any meaningful possibility of knowledge. Quite the contrary, humanists believe that a significant body of reliable knowledge can be arrived at by scientific inquiry, and that thoughtful applications of science and technology can enhance the human condition. Secular humanists wish to extend the methods of science to all areas of human endeavor, in marked contrast to conservative believers who have often conducted unremitting efforts to block scientific research.

Secular humanism is receptive to a wide range of human experiences, including art, morality, poetry, and feeling. Indeed, it is inspired by the arts no less than the sciences. But it is unwilling to declare any belief as validated by private intuitive, mystical, or subjective appeals. Rather validation comes only through the tests of intersubjective confirmation. If intersubjective confirmation is not achievable, then the only reasonable position is to suspend judgment about the hypothesis until such time as we can marshal decisive evidence for or against it. Karl Popper's non-falsifiability principle (that a theory is admissible only if there are conditions under which it can be falsified) has been used against those who propose non-testable claims, particularly in paranormal or religious areas; though others deny that such a line of demarcation can be so easily drawn.

Naturalistic Cosmic Outlook

Naturalists maintain that the universe is intelligible to human reason and explainable by reference to natural causes. This may be

called *scientific naturalism.* The modern secular humanist outlook has been profoundly influenced by naturalism. It looks to the sciences in order to understand nature. What do today's sciences tell us? They describe a world in which physical-chemical processes, matter and energy and their interactions, and the regularities discovered by the natural sciences are primary in the executive order of nature. But nature cannot be reduced simply to its material components; a full account also must deal with the various emergent levels at which matter is organized and functions. Explanations are derived from various contexts under observation. We may approach this on the macro level by reference to our planet and solar system, or to the expanding universe or galaxies (or multiverses) discovered by astronomy, or on the micro level of sub-atomic particles observed by physics and chemistry, or by reference to organic matter in the biosphere explored by the biological sciences. This is sometimes known as "systems theory."

Ever since Charles Darwin in the nineteenth century, evolutionary concepts have become central to our understanding of nature. The theory of evolution seeks to explain the change of species through time in terms of chance mutations,

Charles Darwin

differential reproduction, adaptation, natural selection, and other natural causes. This may very well be called "evolutionary naturalism." Human behavior is thus understood by drawing from many sciences, including biology, genetics, psychology, anthropology, sociology, economics, and other behavioral sciences. The historical sciences help us to interpret the functioning of social institutions and human culture. Any "theories of reality" are thus derived from the tested hypotheses and from theories rooted in scientific inquiry, rather than from poetic, literary, or theological narrations, interesting as these might be.

Naturalists believe that we need to develop, if we can, interdisciplinary integrative generalizations drawn from across the sciences. The concept "coduction" aptly applies. Contrasted with induction and deduction, this means that we *coduce* explanations that cut across scientific disciplines in order to develop a more comprehensive cosmic outlook. E.O. Wilson has used the term "consilience," which he borrowed from the nineteenth century philosopher of science William Whewell. In any case secular humanists need to make every effort to develop a "synoptic perspective," a summing-up, as it were, drawing from many sciences. Secular humanists believe that it is important to convey to the public some understanding of what the sciences tell us about the universe and the place of the human species within it.

This general naturalistic theory avoids materialistic reductionism because it encompasses the system-theoretical insights that emergent phenomena appear at successive levels of complexity which cannot be explained simply in terms of lower-level phenomena, *and* that these nested systems of phenomena themselves constitute a natural phenomenon requiring new hypotheses and theories appropriate to that level. A graphic illustration of this of course is the emergence of countless new species that Darwin discovered on the Galapagos Islands. This does not threaten a naturalistic worldview because it supplements reductive explanations with higher-order explanations, and it does *not* make room for spiritual or mystical explanations. This insight also undergirds the capacity of secular humanism to respond to the bio-world in all its plurality, diversity, and richness; and it leaves room in human culture for science and social institutions, moral justice, and the arts. It also allows us to draw upon human intentions as telenomic explanations of complex psychological behaviors. This approach encompasses both consilience and systems theory. On this interpretation, coduction does not just stretch "horizontally" across disciplinary boundaries, as consilience does; it also stretches "vertically" encompassing the layers of emergent phenomena from the micro to the macro level. It is thus both interdisciplinary and intrasystematic.

This naturalistic perspective of the universe competes with the traditional theological outlook that postulates a supernatural realm, a doctrine of salvation, and an immortal soul, all concepts that scientific naturalists reject.

Non-Theism

Secular humanists are dubious of any effort to divide nature into two realms: the natural and supernatural. They find the classical definition of an omnipotent, omniscient, and beneficent God to be unintelligible, and the alleged proofs for God's existence inconclusive, and the problem of reconciling evil with presumptions of divine justice insurmountable. Arguments from a first cause or unmoved mover are fallacious, for we can

always ask, "Who caused God?" If that question is unanswerable, so also is the question, "Why should there be something rather than nothing?" Highly suspect are the postulations of "fine tuning," "intelligent design" and the "Anthropic Principle." In any case, the theistic belief that God is a "person" represents an anthropomorphic leap of faith that cannot be justified. All such explanations as these are suspect because they transcend nature and hence pose immense, probably insurmountable problems of verification; perhaps the best posture about such questions is that of the skeptic. At the very least we should suspend judgment about the surmised transcendental origins of the universe until such time as such theories can be responsibly and evidentially confirmed or disconfirmed.

Appeals to alleged revelations from God or his emissaries as the basis of religious truths are uncorroborated by competent observers and also highly questionable. The historic claims of revelation of the Abrahamic religions—the Hebrew Bible, the Christian New Testament, the Muslim Qur'an—are not attested to by sufficiently reliable eyewitnesses. Biblical and Qur'anic criticism have shown that these books are not inscribed by God, but are written by fallible human beings; they are the products of apologists for competing faiths. Moreover, if their claimed revelations are taken at face value, they contradict each other. The historical existence of the prophets of the Old Testament such as Moses, Abraham, Isaac, Joseph, and others, is dubious. None of the supposed authors of the New Testament—Mark, Mathew, Luke, John, or even Paul—knew Jesus directly. Nor, with the exception of Paul, were they even written by the men whose names have become attached to them through tradition. These scriptural accounts are second- and third-hand testimony based on an oral tradition that was often contradictory, and in any case merits suspicion because it was conveyed to posterity by propagandists for a new faith. Similarly, the historical accuracy of the Qur'an and Hadith concerning the life of Muhammad is highly suspect, for contrary to Muslim claims that the Qur'an was dictated to Muhammad in a single miraculous event, there is ample historical and textual evidence that there were many different versions of the Qur'an—implying that the Muslim scripture underwent a process of historical development not unlike that of the New Testament.

Basically, secular humanists are *non-*

theists; that is, they find insufficient evidence for belief in God, particularly in the monotheistic sense of God as a person. Some secular humanists have declared that they are outright atheists and have no wish to deny that fact. The difference between nontheists and atheists is that atheists usually define themselves primarily by what they are against, whereas nontheists consider their unbelief to be only part of a broader scientific-philosophical-ethical outlook.

Contemporary secular humanists are also not deists in the eighteenth-century sense, for they do not believe that a divine being created or designed the universe and then left it alone. Still, some secular humanists are not unsympathetic to a Spinozistic conception of the universe in which the regularities or laws of nature inspire an appreciation for its vast magnificence, and this may even elicit a form of "natural piety."

Secular humanists reject any belief in the efficacy of prayer, in the existence of human immortality, or in any hope of receiving salvation from a personal deity. On their view there is insufficient evidence for the claim that the "soul" is separable from the body, that there is a mind-body duality or any "ghost in the machine." All attempts to document an immaterial component to human consciousness, such as the soul, by means of psychical or parapsychological research have thus far been inconclusive. According to neurological science, "consciousness" is most likely a function of the brain and nervous system.

HUMANIST ETHICS

Secular humanism expresses an affirmative set of ethical principles and values. Indeed, some humanists even consider humanist ethics to be its most important characteristic, which should be emphasized in response to religionists, who egregiously maintain that "you cannot be good without belief in God." Humanists hold that ethical values are relative to human experience and need not be derived from theological or metaphysical foundations. Implicit in this is the idea that ethics (like science) is an autonomous field of inquiry. Humanist ethics does not begin or end with meta-ethics—the epistemological analysis of the language of ethical discourse—important as that inquiry is. It focuses instead on concrete conduct in order to make actual normative judgments and recommendations.

"Humanists hold that ethical values are relative to human experience and need not be derived from theological or metaphysical foundations."

The good life is attainable by human beings; and the task of reason is to discover the conditions that enable us to realize happiness. There is some controversy among humanists as to whether happiness involves hedonic pleasure primarily or need-satisfaction, creative growth, and a more elevated contentment such as self-actualization. Hedonism historically drew from Epicureanism, self-actualization theories from Aristotle. Modern hedonism is influenced by utilitarianism, while modern theories of self-realization draw upon humanistic psychology as described by Abraham H. Maslow, Carl Rogers, and Erich Fromm. Humanistic psychologists tend to view human beings as potentially good. They argue that each human's development of moral tendencies depends in part on the nurturing care received by the individual and the satisfaction of biogenic and sociogenic needs (including homeostatic and growth needs, self-respect, love, the experience of belonging to some community, creativity, and the capacity for peak experiences). Many humanists have argued that happiness involves a combination of hedonism *and* creative moral development; that an *exuberant* life fuses excellence and enjoyment, meaning and enrichment, emotion and cognition.

"Many humanists have argued that happiness involves a combination of hedonism and creative moral development; that an exuberant life fuses excellence and enjoyment, meaning and enrichment, emotion and cognition."

Lawrence Kohlberg and Jean Piaget maintained that there are stages of moral growth and development in children and adolescents. Humanists wish to promote such growth in matters of ethics, seeking to elevate the level of taste and appreciation in society. They believe that secular moral education is essential in order to develop the capacity for moral, intellectual, and aesthetic experiences. Moral tendencies have developed in the human species over a long period of evolutionary time; and they are expressed in the development of character and cognition.

> **"Three key humanist virtues are courage, cognition, and caring—not dependence, ignorance, or insensitivity to the needs of others."**

Philosophers from Aristotle through Spinoza, Mill, Dewey, Hook, and John Rawls have argued that ethical choices, at least in part, are amenable to reflective wisdom. Some secular humanists were earlier in the twentieth century sympathetic to emotivism—the view that ethical terms and sentences are subjective and cannot be objectively warranted. This position is now largely discredited, because many ethical judgments are considered to be objectively justifiable. For those who recognize the role of cognition in ethics, deliberation is an essential part of decision-making. During this process value judgments may be appraised in the light of various criteria including our pre-existing values and principles, which may be modified; the causes operative in a problematic situation; the facts of the case before us; means-end considerations; the costs of alternative courses of action; and their consequences.

There is some disagreement between those who maintain that the main test of moral principles should be teleological—that is, judging moral rules by whether they fulfill our long-range ends—or deontological, following Immanuel Kant who maintained that *prima facie,* general moral principles have some independent moral status. Most humanists argue that we should take into account both sets of data—values and ethical principles—though the most important test is consequential and involves an examination of competing claims within a situation. Moral absolutism is rejected as dogmatic and repressive. This position has been labeled "situation ethics" by Joseph Fletcher, and has been attacked as "relativistic" by its critics who claim that it implies a breakdown of all moral standards. Secular humanists deny this, demonstrating that they believe in moral standards but insisting that these grow out of reflective inquiry. They would consider themselves to be *objective* rather than subjective relativists. They also defend naturalistic ethics, the view that moral problems can best be solved by reference to factual knowledge and human experience.

Clearly, naturalists in ethics reject supernatural morality. They maintain that although the classical religious literature may express moral insights, it is often inadequate to the contemporary situation, for it is based upon an earlier (pre-scientific, nomadic and agricultural) level of cultural and moral development. A few examples will suffice to demonstrate this inadequacy. (1) Given belief in the fatherhood of God, any number of moral injunctions may follow concerning the role of women, monogamy, divorce, abortion, war or peace, and the like. It is thus clear that such belief creates no particular moral obligations. (2) Moral obligations do not depend upon divine sanctions or rewards. To do something because of God's commandments, fear of punishment, or hope for reward in the afterlife, is hardly moral; rather, it may impede the development of a mature inner sense of empathy. (3) A whole series of modern critics—Nietzsche, Marx, Freud, and others—have shown that religion may seek to censor truth, repress sexuality, oppose progress, exacerbate human impotence, and offer solace instead of striving to ameliorate the human condition. "No deity will save us, we must save ourselves," says the *Humanist Manifesto II* (1973). We are responsible for our own destiny; we cannot look outside ourselves and our society for succor or salvation.

Three key humanist virtues are courage, cognition, and caring—not dependence, ignorance, or insensitivity to the needs of others. Humanistic ethics therefore focuses on human freedom. It encourages individual growth and development. It focuses on the need of humanists to control their own destinies; to take responsibility, individually and collectively, for their own plans and projects; to enter into the world not simply in order to understand or adore it, but with the intent to use it with prudence to satisfy our needs and desires. Humanistic ethics emphasizes independence, audacity, and resourcefulness. Prometheus can be recognized as the mythical "saint" of humanism, because he is said to have challenged the gods on high, stealing fire and endowing humans with the arts of civilization.

Life presents us with possibilities and opportunities. The meaning of life grows out of what we discover in our own mortal existence; it emerges in our acts of free choice, our goals and aspirations. Insofar as human beings exist for themselves, they are able to define their own realities; they are always in their individual processes of becoming. The salient virtue here is autonomy. Concomitant with this, however, is the recognition that no person can live in total isolation; for humans are social animals. Among the most enduring of human goods are those that we share with others. Some form of altruistic caring is essential to our very being. Developing an appreciation for the common moral decencies (or virtues) and cultivating a general sense of goodwill toward others helps human beings to restrain purely ego-centered interests.

The conflict between self-interest and the social good represents the classical moral paradox. For secular humanists, there may be no easy solutions for some of the dilemmas and tragedies that we encounter in life. Only a reflective decision can best balance competing values and principles, or balance self-interest with the needs and demands of others. Although there are some *prima facie* general guidelines, what we do depends in the last analysis upon the context in which we decide.

Humanist ethics expresses a concern for equality and social justice. Humanists agree with the religious tradition insofar as it supports the idea of the siblinghood of humankind—though not because God commands it, but rather because moral reflection recognizes that we have responsibilities to other human beings. Each individual is to count as equal in dignity and value, an end in himself or herself, entitled to moral considerations; that is the basis or our conception of democracy and human rights, particularly on the global level. We also have some obligation to other forms of sentient life and to other species on the planet Earth.

Sir Karl Popper

Sidney Hook

SOCIO-POLITICAL PERSPECTIVE: DEMOCRATIC HUMANISM

Secular humanism has had a variety of socio-political outlooks during various historical periods. It is concerned throughout with justice and the common good. In the modern world it has emphasized the civic virtues of democracy. There are many sources of the democratic philosophy. John Locke defended human rights, tolerance, and the right of revolution, and John Stuart Mill the right of dissent. In the twentieth century, Sir Karl Popper indicted totalitarian regimes from Plato to Marx and defended pluralistic open democratic societies. John Dewey characterized liberal democracy as a "method of inquiry" engaged in by the public in order to develop sensible policies and elect the officials to carry them out. Dewey wished to rely on educa tion to cultivate an intelligent citizenry able to make informed judgments. Sidney Hook sought to justify democracy on empirical grounds, in the light of its consequences: democratic societies provide more freedom and equality of concern, less duplicity and cruelty, more opportunities for cultural enrichment, creativity, and shared experiences, and higher standards of living. Secular humanists maintain that *political democracy* is essential for a democratic society. The laws and policies of a just government are derived from the "freely given consent" of a majority of the adults voting in elections, with the legal right of opposition, minority rights, due process of law, and civil liberties guaranteed. This is dependent also upon voluntary civic associations and a free press. It presupposes that there is some measure of social equality and free access without racial, ethnic, class, religious, or gender discrimination. It also believes in some measure of economic democracy, in the sense at least that the working population can share in the goods produced by the economy, and that it can through government exercise some democratic control by such means as regulation and taxation.

There has been considerable controversy in the twentieth century between the advocates of economic libertarianism and the proponents of social democracy. The disciples of *laissez faire* such as Ayn Rand wish to limit governmental intrusion in the economy, and maintain that free-market economies are better able than planned economies to achieve growth. Social democrats and liberals believe that the government has an obligation to step in when the private sector is unable to satisfy public needs or the general welfare, and when it violates what they consider to be social justice and the "principles of fairness." Secular humanists recognize that although they may rightly disagree among themselves about any number of specific economic policies, what they share in common is a commitment to the democratic process and the application of reason and science to the solution of social and political problems.

A central controversy that engaged secular humanists throughout the twentieth century was the dispute between liberal democratic humanists and Marxist-Leninists. Western liberal humanists such as Sir Isaiah Berlin and Sidney Hook, and M.N. Roy of

India, emphasized the vital importance of civil liberties and political democracy, asserting that totalitarian Marxist regimes had betrayed the principles of humanism. Some Eastern European Marxist humanists pointed to Marx's youthful *Economic and Philosophical Manuscripts* (1844) with its emphasis on freedom. The vigorous opposition to Stalinism by such thinkers and activists as Svetozar Stojanovic, Ljubomir Tadic, and others helped to blunt the force of totalitarian communism in Eastern Europe.

During the historic battles within democratic societies for equal rights, humanists and secularists, often in alliance with liberal religionists, have generally supported an agenda

Elizabeth Cady Stanton

Betty Friedan

James Farmer

M. N. Roy

of liberation. In the nineteenth century they opposed slavery (Frederick Douglass, Robert Green Ingersoll) and campaigned for women's suffrage (Elizabeth Cady Stanton, Susan B. Anthony). In the twentieth century they supported the battle for feminism (Betty Friedan, Gloria Steinem) and advocated the rights of minorities, blacks (James Farmer, Richard Wright), gays and lesbians, the disadvantaged, and the handicapped.

The continuing battle for democracy has been accompanied by a call for the separation of church and state. The Religious Right in the United States has insisted on making the voice of religion inappropriately prominent in the public square, and it has attempted to secure governmental funding for religious schools and charities. It has sought to mandate the teaching of creationism or intelligent design alongside of evolution in the public schools and has tried to limit the rights of unbelievers. All such measures were opposed by secular humanists. They believe that religion should be a private matter and that the integrity of science should be defended so that students can be exposed to the best science, and that the rights of non-believers be given equal status with believers.

Secular humanists have been especially strong proponents of the *right to privacy.* In questions of medical ethics, this entails support for the right to confidentiality, and to informed consent on the part of patients. It has also been in favor of reproductive freedom, including access to contraception, abortion, and in vitro fertilization. It has also defended the right to die with dignity through such causes as beneficent euthanasia, assisted suicide, and living wills. The right to privacy has been extended to sexual freedom: freedom from undue censorship (entailing the right of adults to publish or read pornographic literature), and of consenting adults to pursue their own sexual proclivities (adultery, sodomy, and same-sex relationships) without repression by the state.

The right of privacy, however, is not defended in isolation from other rights, nor is the relationship of the individual to the social fabric ignored. Although secular humanists emphasize tolerance of competing lifestyles in a pluralistic society, they are not defenders of unbridled libertinism. They advocate the development of excellence and creativity, moderation and self-restraint, prudence and rationality in an individual's personal life, and some sensitivity for the needs of others. They do not wish to legislate private morality, but rather seek by persuasion to develop moral character and ethical rationality.

The secular humanist movement has not confined itself simply to abstract theoretical ideas, but has sought to put its ideas and values into practice. It has endeavored to develop grassroots support by building centers and communities worldwide for non-religious people who are committed to reason, science, free inquiry, secularism, humanist ethics, and democracy. It has focused on education as the best means of developing an appreciation for critical thinking, the naturalistic cosmic outlook, and humanist values.

"The overriding need is 'to develop a new Planetary Humanism' that will seek to preserve human rights and enhance human freedom and dignity"

PLANETARY HUMANISM AND THE NEW PARADIGM

Secular humanists recognize that it is no longer possible for any one nation to solve its problems in isolation from the rest of the world. Interdependence is clearly evident in the areas of trade and commerce, communications and travel, education, culture and science. Unfortunately, severe political, economic, and military competition has often led to war. Religious hatred has likewise engendered violence.

The underlying and unresolved issue the world faces is the use of force by independent nation-states to settle disputes between them. The failure of the League of Nations led to the founding of the United Nations in 1945, at the end of World War II. The problem confronting an exhausted world was how to develop principles of collective security, enabling nations to resolve disputes peacefully without the resort to war. Secular humanists have played an important role in attempting to work out methods of negotiation and compromise on the global scale.

Many humanists were involved in the early days of the United Nations, including Sir Julian Huxley (first head of UNESCO), Sir Loyd Boyd-Orr (head of the World Food Organization), and Brock Chisholm (first Director-General of the World Health Organization). Both the International Humanist and Ethical Union and the Center for Inquiry-*Transnational* have special consultative advisory status within the U.N. as non-governmental organizations. *Humanist Manifesto II*, published in 1973 at the height of the Cold War, deplored the division of humankind on nationalistic grounds.

Humanist Manifesto 2000 (*HM2000*), endorsed by the International Academy of Humanism, provides a "new global agenda" to implement humanist values. It states that the overriding need is "to develop a new Planetary Humanism" that will seek to preserve human rights and enhance human freedom and dignity and will emphasize our commitment "to humanity as a whole." The underlying ethical principle "is the need to respect the dignity and worth of all persons in the world community," Thinkers as diverse as Peter Singer and Hans Küng also emphasize the need for a new global ethic beyond nationalistic, racial, religious, and ethnic chauvinism. *HM2000* sets forth a new "Planetary Bill of Rights and Responsibilities." This includes the recognition that the planetary community has an obligation

United Nations

to do what it can to preserve the global environment and end world hunger, disease, and poverty. National programs of health, welfare, education, ecology, and prosperity now have to be transformed to the transnational level. *HM2000* recommends a set of measures that would strengthen existing UN institutions. But it goes further by calling for an effective new World Parliament elected by the people of the world, not by nation-states; a worldwide security system to resolve military conflicts; an effective world court with enforcement powers; and a transnational environmental protection agency able to preserve the natural ecology and protect other species from extinction. It also recommends an international system of taxation to assist the underdeveloped regions of the world; universal education and healthcare for every person on the planet; some procedures for regulating multinational corporations; a free market of ideas through universal access to the media of communications, which would be neither under the control of nation-states nor global corporations; and some respect for multicultural differences, notwithstanding the need to find common ground for the new planetary civilization that is emerging.

HM2000 concludes with a note of optimism about the human prospect. It rejects theologies or ideologies of despair that look outside of nature for salvation. It affirms that life on the planet Earth can be continually improved and enhanced, provided that human beings are willing to assume responsibility for their own destinies and are willing to undertake cooperative efforts with other men and women of good will to achieve a better future for all.

CONCLUSION

Secular humanism emphasizes the use of reason and critical intelligence to solve human problems. It has confidence in the ability of the human species to apply science and technology for the betterment of human life; it is skeptical of the existence of occult, paranormal, or transcendent realities. Although it is the modern-day version of classical atheism in what it rejects, it also expresses a positive normative concern for developing constructive ethical values relevant to the present conditions of humankind on this planet. It is uncompromising in its commitment to democracy and planetary humanism, and it considers human freedom and fulfillment to be the highest human values. In all of these ways it offers a new paradigm for guiding human life in what might be termed the post-postmodern era.

BIBLIOGRAPHY

Ayer, A. J., ed. *The Humanist Outlook.* London: Pemberton, 1968.

Blackham, H. J. *The Future of Our Past: From Ancient Rome to Global Village.* Amherst, NY: Prometheus Books, 1996.

———. *Humanism.* London: Penguin, 1968.

———, et al. *Objections to Humanism.* London: Penguin, 1974.

Bullock, A. *The Humanist Tradition in the West.* London: Thames & Hudson, 1985.

Davies, T. *Humanism.* London and New York: Routledge, 1997.

Dewey, John. *The Quest for Certainty.* New York: Minton, Balch, 1929.

———. *A Common Faith*, New Haven, CT: Yale University Press, 1934.

Firth, R. *Religion: A Humanist Interpretation.* London: Routledge, 1996.

Flew, Antony. *Atheistic Humanism.* Amherst, NY: Prometheus Books, 1994.

Flynn, Tom. *The New Encyclopedia of Unbelief.* Amherst, NY: Prometheus Books, 2007.

Frolov, I. *Man, Science, Humanism: A New Synthesis.* Amherst, NY: Prometheus Books, 1990.

Goodman, A. and Angus MacKay, eds. *The Impact of Humanism on Western Europe.* London: Longman, 1990.

Hawton, Hector. *The Humanist Revolution.* London: Barre and Rockliff, 1963.

Herrick, Jim. *Humanism: An Introduction.* Amherst, NY: Prometheus Books, 2004.

Hook, Sidney. *The Quest for Being.* New York: St. Martin's Press, 1961.

Humanist Society of Scotland. *The Challenge of Secular Humanism.* Glasgow: Humanist Society of Scotland, 1991.

Huxley, J. *Evolutionary Humanism.* Amherst, NY: Prometheus Books, 1992.

———. *The Humanist Frame.* London: George Allen and Unwin, 1961.

Knight, Margaret. *Humanist Anthology: from Conscious to David Attenborough.* London: Rationalist Press Association, 1961.

Krikorian, Yervant H. *Naturalism and the*

Human Spirit. New York: Columbia University Press, 1944.

Kurtz, Paul. *Eupraxsophy: Living without Religion.* Amherst, NY: Prometheus Books, 1994.

———. *A Secular Humanist Declaration.* Amherst, NY: Prometheus Books, 1980.

———. *Humanist Manifesto 2000.* Amherst, NY: Prometheus Books, 2000.

———. *Humanist Manifestos I and II.* Amherst, NY: Prometheus Books, 1973.

———. *In Defense of Secular Humanism.* Amherst, NY: Prometheus Books, 1984.

———. *Philosophical Essays in Pragmatic Naturalism.* Amherst, NY: Prometheus Books, 1990.

———. *Skepticism and Humanism: The New Paradigm.* New Brunswick, NJ: Transaction Publishers, 2001.

———. *The Transcendental Temptation: A Critique of Religion and the Paranormal.* Amherst, NY: Prometheus Books, 1991.

———, ed. *The Humanist Alternative.* Amherst, NY: Prometheus Books, 1973.

Lamont, Corliss. *The Philosophy of Humanism.* New York: Ungar, 1982.

Popper, Karl. *The Open Society and Its Enemies.*

Princeton, NJ: Princeton University Press, 1971.

Santayana, George. *The Life of Reason.* 5 vols. New York: Scribners, 1905-06.

Sartre, Jean-Paul. *Existentialism and Humanism.* London: Methuen, 1948. First published First published in French in 1946 under the title *L'Existentialisme est un humanisme.*

Smith, J. E. *Quasi Religions: Humanism, Marxism, and Naturalism.* Hampshire, England: Macmillan, 1994.

Smoker, Barbara. *Humanism.* London: National Secular Society, 1984.

Soper, K. *Humanism and Anti-Humanism (Problems of Modern European Thought).* London: Hutchinson, 1986.

Storer, M. *Humanist Ethics: A Dialogue on Basics.* Amherst, NY: Prometheus Books, 1980.

Van Praag, J. P. *Foundations of Humanism.* Amherst, NY: Prometheus Books, 1982.

For further information about Secular Humanism please contact:

The Council for Secular Humansim
PO Box 664
Amherst, NY 14226-9879
716-636-1733
www.secularhumanism.org